MACHINES AT WORK

On the Farm

IAN GRAHAM

QED Publishing

Copyright © QED Publishing 2006

First published in the UK in 2006 by
QED Publishing
A Quarto Group company
226 City Road
London EC1V 2TT
www.qed-publishing.co.uk

A Catalogue record for this book is available from the British Library.

ISBN 978 1 84538 469 2

Written by Ian Graham
Designed by Calcium
Editor Sarah Eason
Foldout illustration Ian Naylor
Picture Researcher Joanne Forrest Smith

Publisher Steve Evans
Editorial Director Jean Coppendale
Art Director Zeta Davies

Printed and bound in China

Picture credits

Key: t = top, b = bottom, c = center, l = left, r = right, FC = front cover

With thanks to **JCB** for photographs for the front cover and pages 3, 7TL, 16BR, 26-27, 30-31, 31TR; **Alamy**/
AG StockUSA/Rick Miller 10-11, /Patrick Eden 13TL, /Patrick Emery 6-7, /Holt Studios/Nigel Cattlin 11TR, /Holt Studios/
Rosie Jordan 4BL, /Profimedia.CZ s.r.o 4-5, /Alan Stone 7CR, /T H Photo 9BL; **Blackthorn Arable Ltd** 12-13 **Corbis**/
Joe Bator 14BC, /Bruce Burkhardt 15BL, /Dean Couger 33TR, /Gehl Co 20BR, 33BL, /Lowell Georgia 31BR, /Lance Nelson
12BC, /Bill Stormont 21-22; **Ecoscene**/Andy Hibbert 25BL, /Peter Landon 22-23; **FLPA**/Richard Becker 22BL, /Nigel Cattlin
28-29, 28CR, /Frans Lanting/Minden Pictures 28BL, /Holt Studios/ Nigel Cattlin 25TR, /Holt Studios/ Nick Spurling 32-33, /
John Tinning 23TR, /Tony Wharton 13BR; **Freefoto**/Ian Britton 14-15, 21TR; **Getty Images** /Colin Raw 7BC;
Still Pictures/Nigel Dickinson 9TR, /Ron Giling 8-9; **USD**/ARS/Bob Nichols 5BL.
Giling 8-9; **USD**/ARS/Bob Nichols 5BL.

Words in **bold** can be found in the Glossary on page 34.

CONTENTS

FARM MACHINES

In the past, people who grew crops and raised animals had few machines to help them. The hard work of pulling heavy **ploughs** and wagons was done by horses or **oxen**. These days, farming is completely different. In many countries, horses and oxen have been replaced by **tractors** and other farm machines. This means that big farms can be run by fewer people – and still produce more food than ever.

Space-age farming

Today, the most advanced farm machines use computers. Computers can give information about how much plant food a crop needs, how wet the soil is and how well crops are growing. Farmers can even track a tractor's exact position on a farm by using radio signals from **satellites**.

◄ Farmers use computer and satellite equipment in their tractors to help them produce bigger and better crops.

▼ Long, curved knives called scythes were once used to cut wheat and grass by hand. On modern farms, **combine harvesters** bring in the wheat crop in a fraction of the time.

tractor

muck spreader

corn harvester

combine harvester

TYPES OF FARM MACHINES

There are all sorts of machines in use on farms today. Tractors pull ploughs and other machines that work the soil, combine harvesters bring in the crops, and cutting machines mow grass and trim hedges.

▲ Farm machines come in all shapes and sizes. Each machine is designed to do a particular job.

TRACTORS

Tractors are probably the most useful of all farm machines. A tractor has big, **grooved** tyres that can grip soft, muddy ground. A powerful engine helps the tractor to pull heavily loaded **trailers**, or drag ploughs behind it through the soil. The driver sits high up in the cab. Big windows give him a clear view all round.

engine exhaust

diesel engine

driver's cab

mudguard

FASTRAC

3220

grooved tyres

FACT!
The **power take-off** (PTO) lets a tractor's engine power another machine, such as a grass cutter, towed by the tractor. It was invented in 1922.

▲ Most farm jobs are done by tractors which is why they are called the workhorses of modern farms.

SPECIAL VEHICLES

Tractors do most of the heavy work on farms, but other vehicles are needed for some jobs. Loaders pile up bales of hay **and straw.**

◀ Even a small loader can lift heavy bales.

Power to spare

Ploughs are machines that can be attached to tractors and used to turn over the soil. Special arms at the back of the tractor can lift the plough clear of the ground when it is not in use.

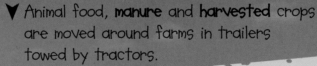

A tractor can raise ▶ and lower a plough.

▼ Animal food, **manure** and **harvested** crops are moved around farms in trailers towed by tractors.

CROSS-COUNTRY

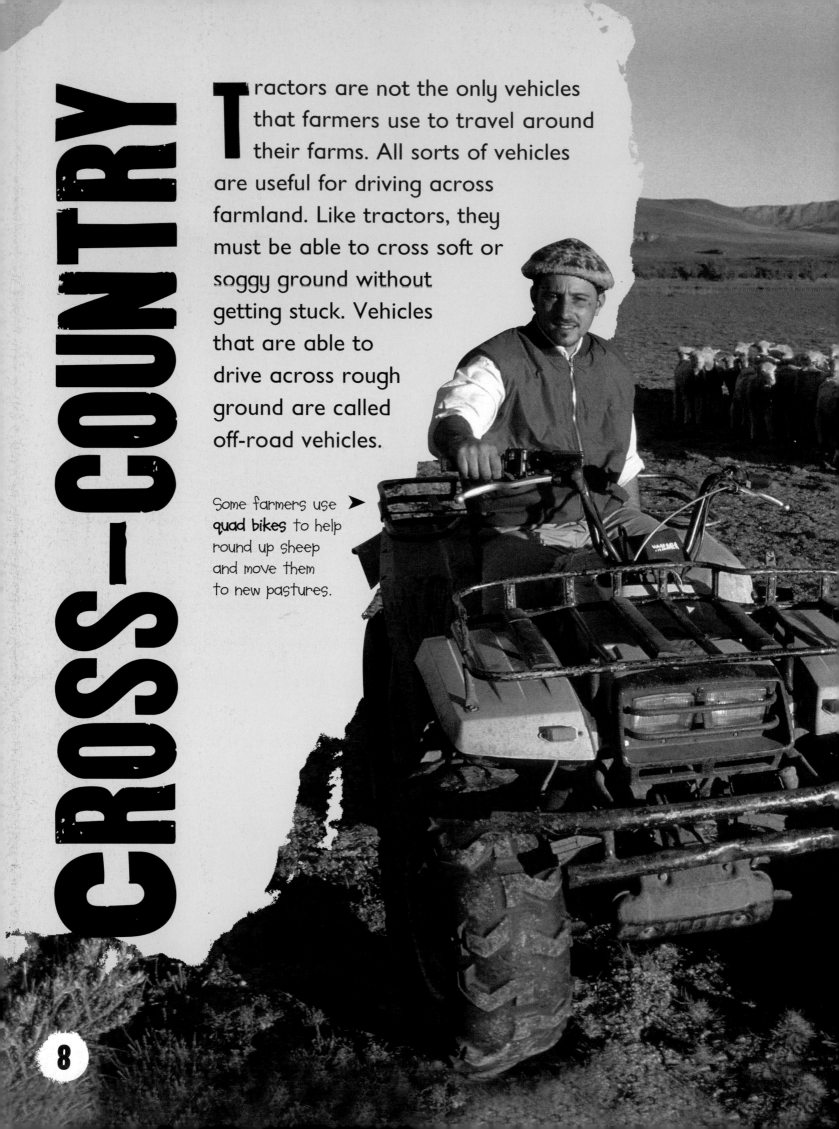

Tractors are not the only vehicles that farmers use to travel around their farms. All sorts of vehicles are useful for driving across farmland. Like tractors, they must be able to cross soft or soggy ground without getting stuck. Vehicles that are able to drive across rough ground are called off-road vehicles.

Some farmers use ➤ **quad bikes** to help round up sheep and move them to new pastures.

FLYING FARMERS

Not all farm vehicles work on the ground. Aircraft are sometimes used for farm work, especially on big farms and cattle ranches in the USA, Canada and Australia. Helicopters are sometimes used to round up cattle and horses on large ranches. The wind from the spinning rotor blades and the noise of the helicopter drive the animals away from it.

▼ A helicopter hovers close to the ground to drive cattle ahead of it.

Four-wheel drive

Ordinary cars do not work well on farms — they easily get stuck on muddy ground. This is because only two of their four wheels are driven by the engine. In off-road vehicles, all four wheels are powered by the engine. This helps them to grip muddy or wet ground.

◄ Four-wheel drive, or off-road, vehicles can travel around farmland almost as well as tractors.

9

Before crops can be planted, the ground must be prepared. The soil surface is broken up to let in air and water. Stirring up the soil also helps to kill weeds. This heavy work is done by machines. Ploughs turn over the soil and **harrows** break it up. Then **cultivators** and **rakes** make a flat, even surface ready for sowing seeds.

Ploughs have a set of curved ➤ blades that slice through the soil and turn it over.

A harrow breaks up big clumps of soil.

Harrows

Harrows are dragged by tractors across ploughed soil to level out the humps and hollows made by the plough. They have **discs**, teeth or spikes to cut through the earth. Harrows are also useful for flattening mole hills.

SPREADING MUCK

Animal waste, also called manure, contains natural plant food that helps grass and crops to grow. It is collected from the farmyard and spread on the ground by a machine called a muck spreader.

▲ As a tractor drives along, a muck spreader flings manure behind it.

PLANTING MACHINES

Once the soil has been prepared, the next job is to plant the crops. It would take too long to sow seeds by hand, so today farmers use machines. Not all seeds sown in open ground grow into healthy plants, however. Many are eaten by birds, or killed by bad weather or disease. Some crops are sown in **glass houses** or plastic tunnels where they can grow in safer conditions. When they have become small plants, called **seedlings**, they are moved out to the fields.

▲ Potato plants are grown from small potatoes called seed potatoes. A potato planting machine pushes the potatoes into piles of soil called ridges.

SOWING SEED

A seed-sowing machine cuts a narrow trench or slit in the soil and then drops seeds into it. The machine plants the seeds in rows. The space left between the rows makes room for machines to come along later and harvest the crop.

seed drill

◄ The machine that sows seeds is called a seed drill.

Planting seedlings

Seedlings are easily damaged and have to be handled carefully. The machines that plant seedlings are called **transplanters**. They have a pair of soft plastic grippers for picking up each seedling. Transplanters make a hole in the ground and then push the seedling into it.

◄ This machine is covering the ground with thin, black plastic. The plastic cover warms the soil, keeps it moist and stops weeds growing. Seedlings are planted through holes in the cover.

LOOKING AFTER CROPS

As crops grow, the young plants must be fed and watered. Plant food, called **fertilizer**, is sprinkled on the soil. Farmers must also make sure the plants have enough water, so if there is not enough rain, the crops have to be watered. Supplying farmland with extra water is called **irrigation**. Chemicals may be sprayed onto crops to kill insects and other pests that might harm them. **Organic** farms look after crops and animals without using **artificial** chemicals.

Aerial work

One way of spraying crops is to do it from the air, using aeroplanes or helicopters. Liquid spray is stored in tanks inside the aircraft and sprayed out of pipes over the crop. The machines that do this work are called crop dusters.

◄ A crop duster swoops low over a crop to spray its chemicals onto the plants.

Floating ➤ harvesters cut and collect underwater weeds to stop them from choking waterways.

COTTON HARVESTERS

Cotton is a crop that is grown in huge quantities and made into clothes. Its fibres grow on the seeds of the cotton plant which are harvested by machines. Some farmers remove the whole seed pod with the cotton fibres still inside, while others take just the cotton fibres.

When tufts of ➤ white fibres burst out of the seed pods of cotton plants, it is time to harvest the crop.

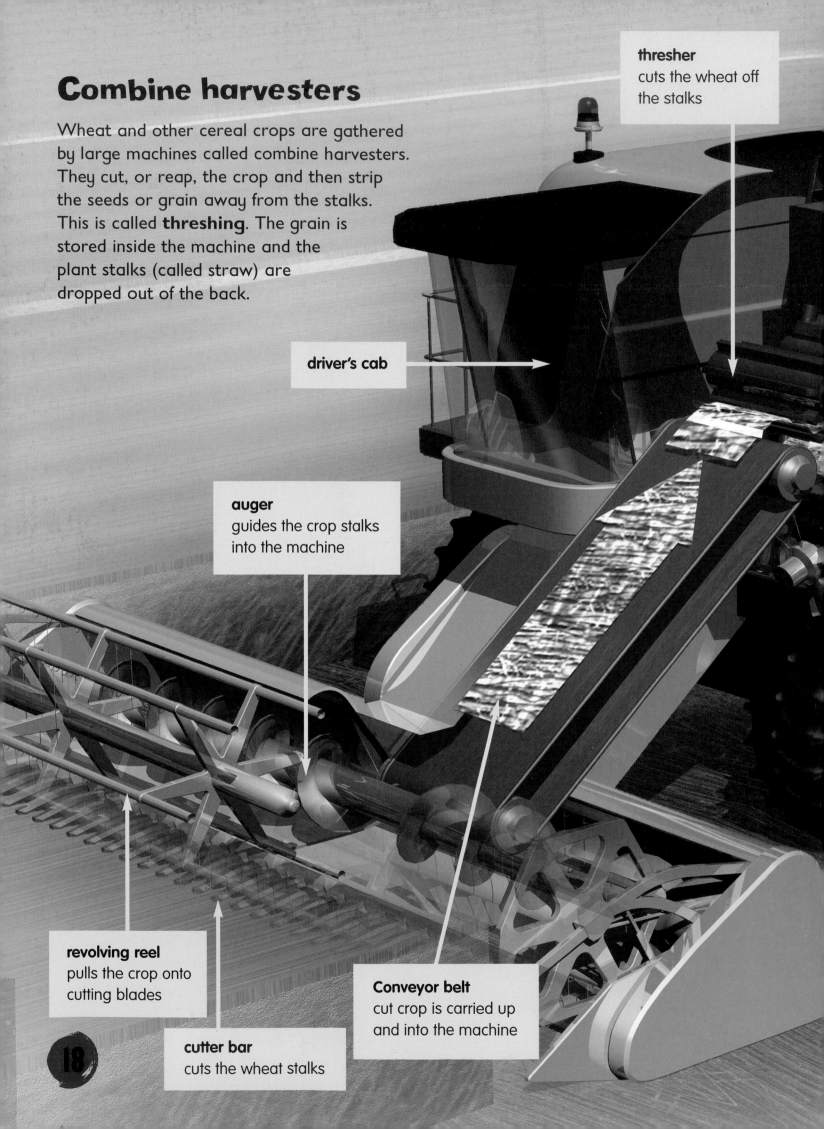

Combine harvesters

Wheat and other cereal crops are gathered by large machines called combine harvesters. They cut, or reap, the crop and then strip the seeds or grain away from the stalks. This is called **threshing**. The grain is stored inside the machine and the plant stalks (called straw) are dropped out of the back.

thresher
cuts the wheat off the stalks

driver's cab

auger
guides the crop stalks into the machine

revolving reel
pulls the crop onto cutting blades

Conveyor belt
cut crop is carried up and into the machine

cutter bar
cuts the wheat stalks

Collecting grass

Grass is gathered by a machine called a **forage harvester**. It picks the cut grass up off the ground and blows it through a long curved spout into a trailer that is driven alongside the harvester.

▲ A forage harvester collects grass that will be made into hay.

▲ Harvest time is the busiest time of the year on a farm. Machines help farmers to harvest crops quickly.

CUTTERS

Farm fields are often surrounded by hedges, which have to be cut back regularly to stop them growing too big. Tall hedges cast long shadows that stop light reaching nearby plants. Wide hedges take up space in which crops could grow. Garden hedges can be cut with small hand trimmers, but farm hedges are bigger and longer and must be cut with bigger machines.

Power Arm 95

blades

JOHN DEERE

▲ A mowing machine has razor-sharp blades for cutting grass.

GRASS CUTTING

Grass is an important food for farm animals. During the summer, they eat lush, fresh grass in the fields. Grass does not grow in the winter, so sheep and cattle are given hay to eat instead. Hay is long grass which is cut and dried in the summer. Green plants can also be cut and stored to make a food called silage. Grass is cut by machines called mowers.

Trimming trees

Trees are cut back using chain saws. A small engine drives a metal chain round and round the edge of a long flat metal blade. The fast-moving chain has sharp teeth that cut through the wood.

A chain saw can cut ➤ through thick branches and tree trunks quickly and easily.

◄ A hedge—cutting machine on the end of a tractor's **mechanical** arm is used to keep farm hedges neatly trimmed.

23

GLASS HOUSES

Most crops are grown in fields, but some grow better if they are protected from the wind, rain and cold. These plants are grown inside glass houses or **greenhouses**. If the buildings are heated, they are sometimes called hothouses. Some glass houses just keep the weather out, but others are space-age growing machines! Inside them, the temperature, watering, air moisture and even the amount of light are all controlled by computers.

Farmers can grow better quality crops, ▼ such as tomatoes and lettuces, in greenhouses and glass houses.

AIR AND WATER

A mist of fine water droplets is sprayed over plants in a greenhouse if the air dries out too much. The soil is kept damp by the correct amount of watering. Nutrients **are dissolved in the water to feed the plants.**

Greenhouse crops, like these ➤ pepper plants, are watered by pipes buried in the soil.

Heat and light

Heaters warm the air in greenhouses to keep plants at the right temperature. Fans blow the warm air through the building. Lamps provide extra light if there is not enough sunlight. When it is cold and dull outside, extra heating and lighting can make crops grow for longer periods of time.

▲ If the air inside a greenhouse cools too much, heaters automatically switch on.

25

LIFTERS

Lifting hay bales and other heavy materials is hard work, which is why farmers use machines to do the job. Some tractors can have a big wide bucket, called a **loader** bucket, fitted to their front. This is useful for scooping things up off the ground. The **telehandler** is a different kind of lifting machine. Its name means 'telescopic handler'. It uses a long arm, called a **boom**, to lift things.

A telehandler's ➤ boom is a useful tool. It can reach forwards as well as lift things.

Attachments

Telehandlers and other farm lifting machines can be fitted with **attachments** for different jobs. There are spikes, forks and grabs for lifting hay bales, and buckets for lifting all sorts of materials.

◄ This telehandler is fitted with a fork and grab attachment for gripping hay bales.

▼ Fork attachments are useful for stacking bales of hay and straw.

FORKLIFT TRUCKS

A forklift truck has long prongs at the front that can be moved up and down. The prongs are very strong and can lift crates, bales and other heavy objects.

LOOKING AFTER ANIMALS

Most of the machines used on farms with animals are the same tractors, trailers, loaders and **diggers** that are used on non-animal farms. However, there are a few machines that are specially designed for looking after animals, such as milking machines. At one time cows were milked by hand, which was a long, slow process. Today, cows are milked by machines that copy the sucking action of calves.

Milking machines

Before milking begins, the cow's **udder** is washed. All the milk collected from the cow is pumped into a tank and chilled to keep it fresh.

Four tubes called a cluster gently ➤ suck milk out of each cow's udder, in the same way a feeding calf would.

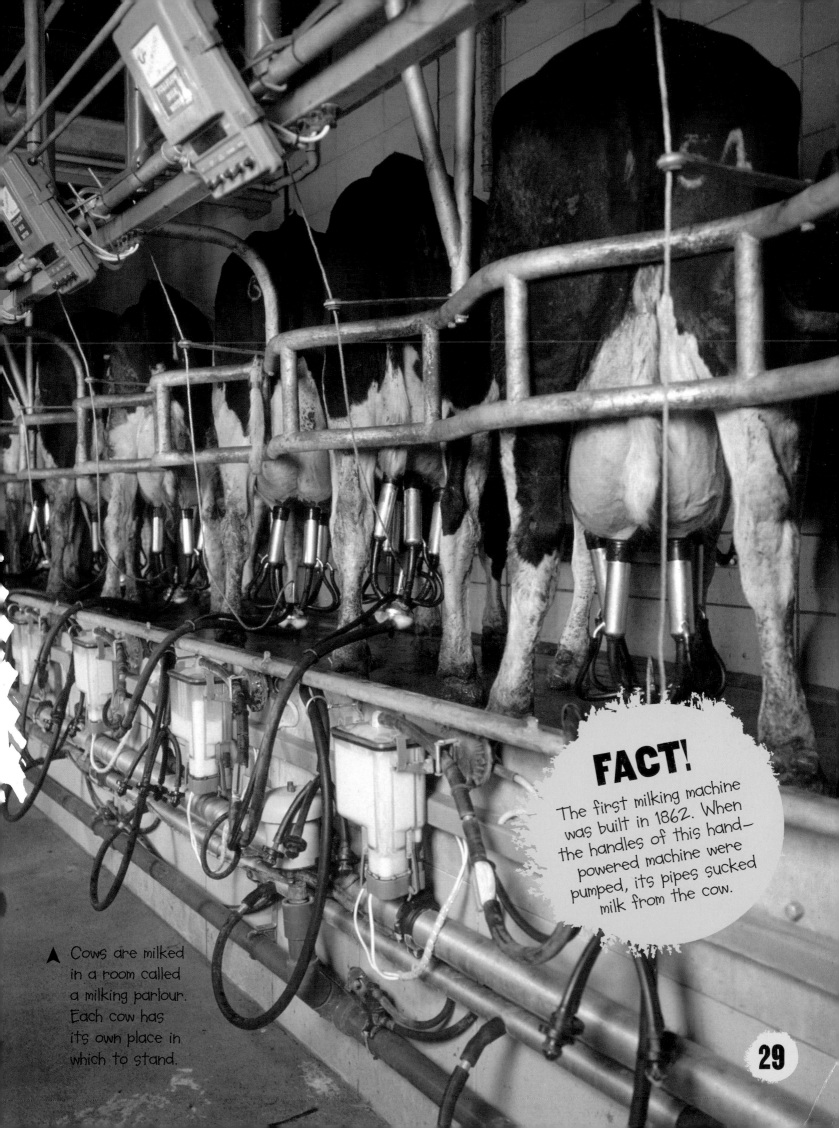

FACT!
The first milking machine was built in 1862. When the handles of this hand—powered machine were pumped, its pipes sucked milk from the cow.

▲ Cows are milked in a room called a milking parlour. Each cow has its own place in which to stand.

DIGGERS

Holes are dug on farms by many different types of machine. Lots of them are the same as machines used on building sites. They have a mechanical arm with a bucket on the end. The arm pushes the bucket into the ground. Teeth along the edge of the bucket help to break up the earth and scoop it up. There are even machines that make holes for fence posts and trenches for drains.

The **backhoe loader** is a ▶ digging machine. It has a small bucket at the back for digging and a wide bucket at the front for scooping and loading.

Post work

Machines are also used on farms to put up fences. **Post-hole borers** drill holes into the ground to hold fence posts. If the ground is not too hard, machines called **post drivers** can hammer the posts straight into the ground.

▲ A post-hole borer is screwed into the ground and pulled out again to make a neat hole for a fence post.

DIGGING DRAINS

Soggy soil is bad for plants because it rots their roots. One way to dry out wet land is to dig narrow slots with a trenching machine and lay drains at the bottom. Another way is to use a machine called a mole plough to cut channels under the ground for water to drain into.

◄ A trenching machine slices through the ground and makes a long narrow hole in which drains can be laid.

31

TRUCKS

A lot of heavy materials have to be transported to and from farms. Supplies such as fertilizer and animal food are delivered, and harvested crops are taken away for sale. Milk must be collected from dairy farms every day, and animals such as cattle and sheep need to be taken to and from market. Some of the biggest trucks on the roads do this work.

Milk tankers are made from ➤ stainless steel, because it will not rust and spoil the milk.

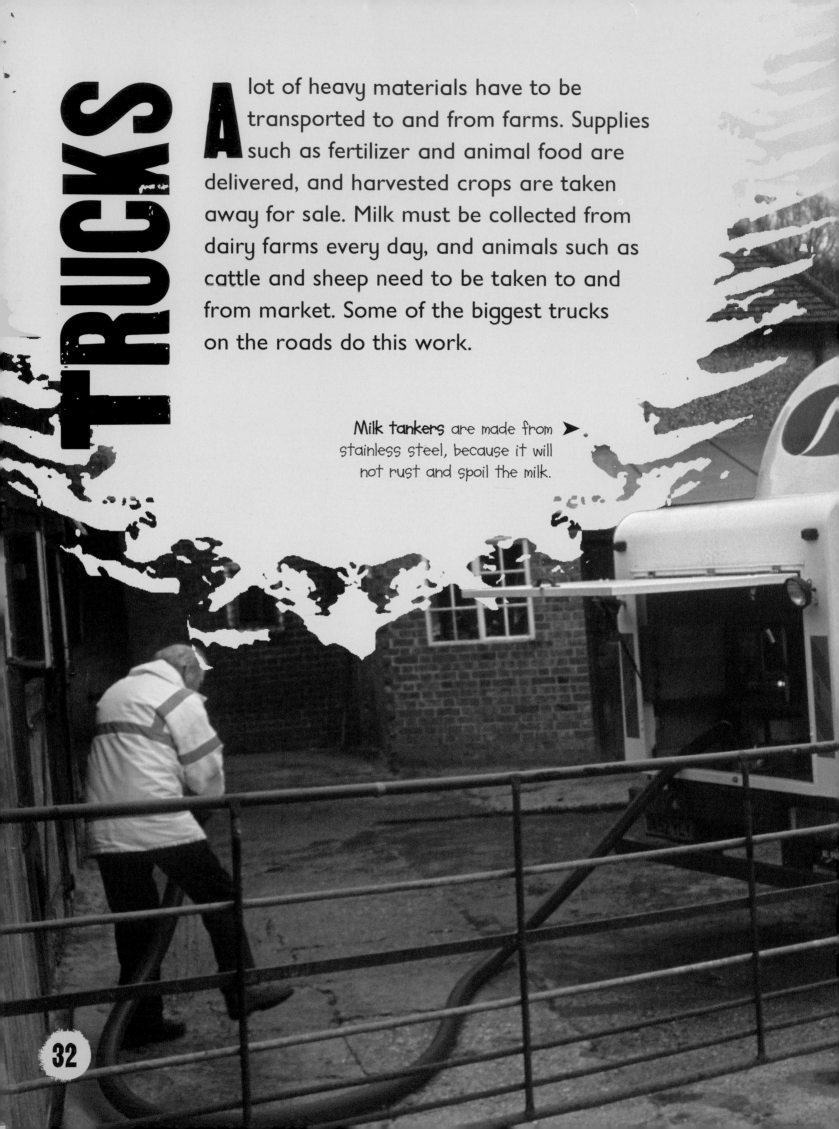

A moving belt loader fills a truck with harvested potatoes. The top end of the belt can be moved up or down to the right height for the truck. ➤

Dump trucks

Many of the trucks that do the heavy transport work in the farming industry are dump trucks. They are filled up by a machine called a loader, or by a moving belt. Then, to empty its load, the back of the truck tips up and everything inside slides out.

◄ Dump trucks collect all sorts of harvested crops from farms.

GLOSSARY

artificial something that is man-made and not found naturally

attachment a piece of machinery that can be attached to another machine. A plough is an attachment that can be linked up to a tractor

backhoe loader a digging machine with a mechanical arm that has a bucket on the end

bale a bundle of hay, straw, cotton or other plant material

baling machine a machine that collects hay or straw together into large bundles or bales

boom a metal arm

combine harvester a farm machine that cuts crops such as wheat or barley and separates the grain (seeds) from the stalks

cultivator a farm machine that stirs up the top layer of soil

digger a machine with a bucket that can dig up large amounts of soil or other materials

disc something that is circular in shape. Metal discs are found on harrows and are used to cut through the soil

fertilizer a mixture that is added to soil to feed plants

forage harvester a farm machine that picks up hay or plant stalks. They are then blown out of a chute into a wagon and made into silage

glass houses buildings made almost entirely from glass. Crops that need a lot of warmth and sunlight are grown in glass houses

greenhouses like glass houses, buildings made from glass in which crops that need a lot of warmth and sunlight are grown

grooved a surface that has hollows between raised areas

harrow a farm machine pulled by a tractor that uses discs or spikes to break up clumps of soil. Harrows are used to flatten the soil

harvested cut and collected crops

hay grass that has been cut and dried

irrigation a system of cutting channels into the ground that lead from a water supply to crops. Irrigation is used to keep crops watered at all times

loader a machine with a big bucket at the front that can scoop up materials and load them into a truck

manure a natural material spread onto the land to feed plants. Animal waste is often used as manure

mechanical something that is worked by a machine

milk tanker a vehicle with a large container in which milk is transported from dairy farms

mower a machine that cuts grass

nutrients vitamins and minerals that keep plants and animals healthy

organic something grown without the use of artificial chemicals

oxen male cattle

plough a farm machine pulled by a tractor to turn over the top of the soil

post driver a machine that is used to knock posts firmly into the ground

post-hole borer a machine that is used to cut round holes into the ground into which posts can be placed

power take-off (PTO) part of a farm tractor that supplies engine power to another machine

prong a long, narrow instrument with a sharp, pointed end

quad bike a small motorbike with four wheels. Quad bikes are sometimes used for getting around farms or helping to round up animals

rake a piece of equipment with a number of sharp spikes. Pulling a rake across the ground sweeps up mown grass or plant stalks. Farm rakes are pulled by tractors

rotor blades the metal blades found on a helicopter that turn to make it take off

satellite a machine that travels in space around the world and sends signals back to Earth

seedling a very young plant

silage animal food that is made from green plants

swather a farm machine that cuts crops and bundles them into windrows

telehandler a farm vehicle with an extending boom, or arm, for lifting heavy loads such as hay bales

threshing separating the seeds of a crop such as wheat from the rest of the plant

tractor a farm vehicle used for pulling trailers and machines

trailer a container with four wheels that is attached to a tractor and pulled behind it

transplanter a machine that puts small plants in the ground, one by one

trench a long, narrow cut in the ground

udder the part of a cow in which milk is made

windrow a long, low ridge or row of hay

FIND OUT MORE

Websites

Go on a virtual tour of a dairy farm:
http://www.hants.gov.uk/sparsholtschoolscentre/photovisit/pv_totd.html

Discover how milk gets from the farm to you:
http://www.mda.state.mi.us/kids/pictures/dairy

Find out about farming and agriculture:
http://www.kids.net.au/encyclopedia-wiki/ag/Agriculture

Fun, games and quizzes about farming:
http://www.johndeerekids.com/home.html

Find out more about farms and farm animals:
http://www.agr.state.il.us/kidspage

INDEX